Bottoms Up!

"Lean forward into life"
(*A favorite axiom of Irving Johnson*)

Books By Robert McKenna

The Dictionary of Nautical Literacy

Bottoms Up!

**Toasts, Tales & Traditions of
Drinking's Long History as a Nautical Pastime**

Concocted by
ROBERT McKENNA

FLAT HAMMOCK PRESS
MYSTIC, CONNECTICUT

Flat Hammock Press
5 Church Street
Mystic, CT 06355
www.flathammockpress.com

Library of Congress Cataloging-in-Publication Data

McKenna, Robert.
  Bottoms up! : toasts, tales & traditions of drinking's long history
as a nautical pastime / by Robert McKenna.
     p. cm.
  ISBN 0-9758699-2-2
  1. Toasts. 2. Sea proverbs. 3. Sailing—Miscellanea. I. Title.
  PN6341.M35 2005
  082—dc22

                                        2004030603

Printed in U.S.A.
Illustrations © Deborah McLaren

To friends…
life's anchor and compass

Acknowledgments

To Captain Bob Bates, William Barnum, Jim Cassidy,
Barbara Caulkins, Mark Entwistle, Steve Finnegan,
Donald Demers, Gordon Ghareeb, Kelly Hall, Geoff Jones,
Greta Jones, Steve Jones, Allen Kruger, Jim Lynch,
Tamara McKenna, Mark & Beth Robinson, Danny Spear,
Kurt Volkan, Lou Vinciguerra, Ty Whitman…

SKÅL!

*(This Swedish toast came from the Viking practice of
drinking ale from the skulls of defeated enemies.)*

Author's Note

A good toast should be a gift. It should be appropriate for the occasion, positive, sincere and, ideally, memorable. In my experience, a well-made toast has the ability to fix a special moment in time.

The intent of this slim volume is not to glorify the act of drinking, but to emphasize that every occasion we share with others can be made that much more special with a simple toast.

At times we all have trouble finding the right words, how to say them, and when. As my professional and recreational pursuits largely revolve around the sea, I thought it appropriate to compile a "sheet anchor" for fellow mariners, boaters, sailors, fishermen and coastal dwellers.

Every effort has been made to verify the accurate wording and proper attribution to the toasts and quotes included in this book. If an entry has no attribution then the source is unknown, uncertain or anonymous.

Should there be any omissions or improperly credited material in this book, I wish to express now my deep regret. Corrections and/or additions may be sent along to the publisher.

Please remember, spontaneity has its time and place... and no time is better for a toast than when together with friends and loved ones. So, grab your conch shell and give a call, light the tiki torches, and mix a Mai-Tai for me!

My best wishes go along with a dip of the ensign.

Robert McKenna, 2005
– Noank, Connecticut

The phrase "Bottoms Up!" is believed to have its origin in the practice of drinking from glasses fashioned with round bottoms and no stem (such glasses were commonplace aboard ships at sea). These glasses had to be drained "bottoms up" lest they tumble over and spill their cargo. These glasses were the forerunners and namesakes of today's tumblers.

Table of Contents

Cheers — a salutation before drinking.
The nautical equivalent could very well be *"Huzza."*

Introduction

A float or ashore, saltwater or fresh, power or sail, salty dog or landlubber, frozen, mixed or straight up, the ultimate destination for many of us is happy hour. In fact, the term "happy hour" is said to have originated in the U.S. Navy as a scheduled period of time for entertainment and refreshment.

The prudent mariner will always have two or three short toasts in his or her sea bag for when the opportunity presents itself. Whether it's docktails at a quiet gathering in the slip, meeting mates at a waterfront watering hole, sampling marine cuisine at a raft or deck party, addressing a sea of blue-blazers at the yacht club, or hobnobbing at a bubbly bon-voyage bash, the ability to raise a wise, witty or clever toast is a time-honored seafaring social custom and a true art form.

Bottoms Up! is the ideal crewmate and a perfect drinking companion. In addition to nautical toasts, it includes proverbs, slogans, sayings and quotes that can be spun into a gracious gesture suitable for any occasion. It is brimming with fun facts and garnished with amusing anecdotes that will charm your guests and make you the host—with the toast—that pleases the most.

Pipe "up spirits." Knock off ship's work. Grab some rocks from your diver's helmet ice bucket, reach into the globe bar for your ship's decanter, pour your favorite libation to the Plimsoll mark in your most beloved drinking vessel and make an offering to King Neptune.

"Bottoms Up!"—or as former Soviet president Mikhail Gorbachev, trying his best to impress an English-speaking audience, once said, "Up your bottoms!"

aqua vitae — "water of life"

Nautical Toasts

Toasting or the raising of glasses in tribute to an individual or an institution, as a measure of respect, is a social custom that dates to antiquity.

By many accounts, drinking to one's health was initiated by the ancient Greeks as a way for a host to assure others that the wine they were drinking was not poisoned.

It is from the Romans that we have the word "toast." They dropped pieces of burnt bread into wine to improve the flavor. Subsequently, the Latin *tostus*, meaning roasted or parched, came to mean the drink. This practice of floating croutons continued into the 1600s when along the waterfronts of Europe, seamen customarily placed a small piece of toast in their ale or mulled wine. Once saturated, the toast would sink to the bottom of the goblet. Soon enough, someone would challenge "Toast!" and a race was on to see who could drain their goblet first and eat the toast. While perhaps more palatable than an agave worm, the glob of soggy bread would often miss the mouth. This became known as "mud in your eye!"

Toasts that expressed heart-felt sentiments were

readily adopted to help eliminate alcohol's negative stigma, and the custom of toasting went to sea with Britain's Royal Navy, which essentially saw them as drinking-based salutes. The Royal Navy even devised a formal toast for every day of the week, thus reinforcing its place as a maritime ritual.

Over the centuries toasts entered all sectors of society, and today they are most common at weddings, military ceremonies, ship christenings, formal state functions—and nickel-beer night at the corner pub.

Trading toasts—the ultimate "liquid pro quo"

Time-Tested Toastmaking Tips

M astering the ability to offer a toast can turn even the simplest of occasions into a memorable event. Today we only think of offering a toast at weddings and other formal events. Toasts, however, are appropriate any time good friends get together socially.

A toast offered at the outset of a voyage, project or new endeavor—a traditional anointment of good luck—is also appropriate. All that's needed to make a good toast (in addition to a measure of festive beverage) is a little forethought, practice and some basic etiquette and protocol.

If you're a guest, don't propose a toast until the host, or someone designated by the host, has had an opportunity to do so. If you'd like to propose a toast, ask the host first. Be sure that your glass and all others are charged... no one likes low tide. It's also polite to remove your hat, if you're wearing one.

When making a toast always raise your glass with your right hand (unless it's a hook) and hold your arm straight from your shoulder. Look at the person being toasted while speaking. Keep it short. Witty is good, but remember, as Polonius said in *Hamlet*, "Brevity is the soul of wit." If you're the one being toasted, don't stand, raise your glass or drink. Do thank the toasters (a smile or nod will do). Toasts can be sealed with champagne, wine, mixed drinks or non-alcoholic punch (coffee, tea, or water are certainly acceptable when underway).

It is also acceptable to strike your glass with your spoon to get everyone's attention. It's okay but not necessary to clink glasses. The practice of clinking glasses goes back to ancient times, and was thought to ward off evil spirits. If toasting in someone's memory, it is not appropriate to touch glasses.

It is considered disrespectful for an individual not to participate in a toast. A non-drinker need only go through the motion of holding the glass to his or her lips or request a non-alcoholic beverage. Other customs include linking arms when drinking and beating the table in applause.

It's not wise to drink excessively before a toast for Dutch courage, "lest one's slurring be more incomprehensible than a stuttering Billy Budd."

Toasts are often rendered to each branch of the Armed Services, and if a member (or former member) of that branch is present he or she should receive the toast. Another old navy custom is to respond to a toast by draining the glass and throwing it over the left shoulder so that no lesser toast be drunk. And lastly, the final toast of any gathering should be drained.

Toasts

May the ships at sea never be bottoms up.

Aaaaaarrrrrgh!
—*pirate toast*

To those at sea.
—*traditional third toast*

To the (vessel name) and her crew.

God bless this ship and all who sail in her.

May the warm wind at your back not be your own.

From rock and sands and every ill,
May God preserve the sailor still.

If you drink like a fish, drink what a fish drinks!

Nowhere is too far.
—*motto of the Cruising Club of America*

Here's to matrimony…
The high sea for which no compass
has yet been invented.

May your voyage through life be as happy and as free
As the dancing waves on the deep blue sea.
or
May your life together be as happy and free,
As the rolling waves on the deep blue sea.

Our (my) wake is your funeral!

Non sibi sed patriae!
(Not for self, but country)
—*unofficial U.S. Navy motto*

To whatever floats your boat

May no son of the ocean be devoured by his mother.
—*navy toast*

A rising tide floats all boats.

In Peace and War
—*U.S. Merchant Marine motto*

Here's to the men of the navy
who sail the ocean blue.
They man our ships, guard our land
and to our flag are true.
—*navy toast*

Got Wind?

To youth and freedom!
—*pirate toast*

I wish you health, I wish you well,
and happiness galore.
I wish you luck for you and friends;
what could I wish you more?
May your joys be as deep as the oceans,
your troubles as light as its foam.
And may you find, sweet peace of mind,
wherever you may roam.

Grog, grub and glory.
—*navy toast*

Down the hatch!

Gold ships, fair winds, and brave seamen.
—*navy toast*

Part went for liquor, part went for women
and the rest I spent foolishly...
—*a sailor's response to what happened to his paycheck*

Marriage is a lot like the navy, everyone complains,
but you'd be surprised at the large number that re-enlist.

Here's to the ships of our navy
And the ladies of the land;
May the first be ever well-rigged,
And the latter ever well-manned.
—*navy toast*

True hearts and sound bottoms.
—*navy toast*

Take care of the ship and the ship will take care of you.

To better times and a speedy calm to the storms of life.

Sailors... Wolves in ship's clothing

A stout ship, a clear sea,
and a far-off coast in stormy weather.
—*navy toast*

It takes three years to build a ship
but three hundred years to build a tradition.
—*Royal Navy axiom*

NAVY — Never Again Volunteer Yourself

The difficult we do now…
the impossible takes a little longer!
—*SeaBee slogan*

Cruising… fixing your boat in exotic places.

Can Do!
—*SeaBee motto*

Fair winds and following seas
or
Fair winds and following seas
and long may your big jib draw!
—*naval blessing*

If there is no wind, row.

To our country! Lift your glasses!
To its sun-capped mountain passes,
To its forest, to its streams
To its memories, to its dreams.

Constriumus, Batuimus
(We Build, We Fight)
—*SeaBee motto*

It's not the towering sail,
but the unseen wind that moves the ship.

I should go down to the sea again,
but it sets me all a quiver.
The seas' call is a wild call—
that's why I stay in the river.

May the clouds in your life form only a background
for a lovely sunset.

We cannot direct the wind…
but we can adjust the sails.

Semper Paratus
(Always Ready)
—*U.S. Coast Guard motto*

You are my anchor to windward.

Once you sail upon the sea,
float on the breeze, ride on the waves,
your life is changed forever.

The only easy day was yesterday.
—*U.S. Navy SEALs motto*

When you drink from a stream remember the spring.

Shiver my timbers!

God promises a safe landing but not a safe passage.

The watch is changed,
The glass is running.
We shall have a good voyage
If God is willing.

The hasty and the tardy meet at the ferry.

Ex Scientia Tridens
(From Knowledge, Seapower)
—*U.S. Naval Academy motto*

The weather is here, wish you were beautiful!
—*old postcard saying*

He that would go to sea for pleasure
would go to hell for a pastime.

Acta non verba
(Deeds, not words)
—*U.S. Merchant Marine Academy motto*

Give a man a fish, and you'll feed him for a day;
give him a religion,
and he'll starve to death while praying for a fish.

Nothing makes a fish bigger than almost being caught.

Land is nothing more than a navigational hazard.

If it moves, salute it. If it doesn't move, pick it up.
If you can't pick it up, paint it.
—*U.S. Navy saying*

Even a fish wouldn't get into trouble
if he kept his mouth shut.

Here's to your new boat and mine—
May they never accidentally meet.

May the sunshine of comfort
dispel the clouds of despair.

Here's to the loved ones we left behind
Out of sight but never out of mind.

To Neptune for a safe voyage.

There are old skippers, and there are bold skippers,
but there are no old bold skippers.

Scientiae Cedit Mare
(The Sea Yields to Knowledge)
—*U.S. Coast Guard Academy motto*

May your departures equal your landfalls.

Sailing: The fine art of getting cold and wet while
slowly going nowhere at great expense.

A boat is a hole in the water
into which one pours money.

Don't rock the boat.

Mal de Mer – French for "you can't take it with you."

Dear Lord,
Be good to me… The sea is so wide
And my boat is so small.
—*Irish fisherman's prayer*

A small hole could sink a great ship.

Any fool can go to sea,
but it's getting back into the harbor that counts.

Here's to learning the ropes without coming unraveled.

The wind that blows,
the ship that goes
And the lass that loves the sailor.
—*Old English saying, popular toast used in England about 1820*

The good seaman is known in bad weather.

From the boat we get to the ship.

The meek shall inherit the earth,
the brave will get the oceans.

The only cure for seasickness
is to sit on the shady side of an old church
in the country.

True sailors die on the turn of the tide,
Going out with the ebb.

Long may she ride, our Navy's pride,
And spur to resolution
And seamen boast, and landsmen toast,
The Frigate *Constitution*.
—*U.S. Navy song*

Bragging may not bring happiness, but no man having
caught a large fish goes home through an alley.

God is good but never dance in a small boat.

May you always have water under your keel.

May your life be as beautiful as a summer day,
with just enough clouds
to make you appreciate the sunshine.

Life's a reach; Then you gybe.

Nodding the head does not row the boat.

Sail Fast... Live Slow!

May all your joys be pure joys,
And all your pain champagne.

History flows forward on rivers of beer.

When in doubt, let it out.

Born to sail. Forced to work.

Here's to the land we love and the love we land.

The first in the boat has the choice of oars.

Got Bait?

May there always be water under your boat,
May she always be seaworthy and ever afloat,
May your bilge pump be certain to work all night and all day,
May your compass and charts always show the safe way,
May you find gentle harbor as every day ends,
May you lower your anchor amidst peace and good friends.
—*A boater's blessing*

We're out here on the sea's sufferance—not as equals,
certainly not as challengers.
Because the sea can't lose. Only we can lose.

It's not just a Jibe, it's an Adventure!

Sailing: Hours of absolute boredom
punctuated with moments of sheer terror.

Water can float a boat or sink it.

An angler is a man who spends rainy days sitting
around on the muddy banks of rivers doing nothing
because his wife won't let him do it at home.

There's more to life than sailing…
And when you find it let me know!

One hand for the ship, one hand for yourself.
—a reason why a sailor is referred to as a "hand."

Powerboaters are always trying to get somewhere…
sailors are already there!

A sea wind changes less often
than the mind of a weak man.

Semper Appotus
(always intoxicated)

Navigation is what tells you where you are,
even when you aren't.

Taking the line of least resistance still makes both
men and rivers crooked.

It's easy to drift, with the current swift.
Just lie in your boat and dream.
But in nature's plan, it takes a real man [or woman],
to paddle the boat upstream.

Give a man a fish and he will eat for a day.
Teach him how to fish, and he will sit in a boat
and drink beer all day.

Give a man a fish, he eats for a day.
Give a man a boat, he cannot afford to eat again.

Carpe Glass
(seize the glass)

The water is the same on both sides of the boat.

May the winds of fortune sail you,
May you sail a gentle sea.
May it always be the other guy
who says, "this drink's on me."

I'd rather be a sailor and sail before the mast
than be a lousy 2nd mate and kiss the captain's ass.

For every wound, a balm.
For every sorrow, cheer.
For every storm, a calm.
For every thirst, a beer.

May you have the health of a salmon,
A strong heart, and a wet mouth.

To a poor sailor, every wind is against him.

A drunk sailor aloft in a storm is a dead sailor.

When the tide of life turns against you,
and the current upsets your boat.
Don't waste time on what might have been,
Just lie on your back and float.

A drowning man will catch at a straw.

Better drunk than drowned.

When the river is deepest it makes least noise.

He who has not yet reached the opposite shore
should not make fun of him who is drowning.

Everything I need to know about life, I learned from
Noah's Ark:
One: Don't miss the boat.
Two: Remember that we are all in the same boat.
Three: Plan ahead.
It wasn't raining when Noah built the Ark.
Four: Stay fit. When you're 600 years old,
someone may ask you to do something really big.
Five: Don't listen to critics;
just get on with the job that needs to be done.
Six: Build your future on high ground.
Seven: For safety's sake, travel in pairs.
Eight: Speed isn't always an advantage.
The snails were on board with the cheetahs.
Nine: When you're stressed, float a while.
Ten: Remember, the Ark was built by amateurs;
the *Titanic* by professionals.

It takes a strong man to swim against the current;
dead fish will float with it.

Deviate an inch, lose a thousand miles.

Don't wait for your ship to come in; swim out to it.

If the ocean were a goblet
And all its salt seas wine,
I would drink it to you darlin',
Ere you cross the foamy brine;
For then you couldn't cross it,
But would have to stay on land
Till the walkin' should get better,
And we'd cross it hand in hand.

Here's to tall ships
Here's to small ships
Here's to all the ships on the sea
But the best ships are friendships
Here's to you and me.
or
There are good ships, and there are wood ships,
The ships that sail the sea.
But the best ships, are friendships,
And may they always be.

The person rowing the boat seldom has time to rock it.

Friends may come and friends may go,
Friends may sail away you know,
Though friends will stick through thick and thin,
Sail on out and sail back in...

Follow the river and you will find the sea

Women and children first!
—*precedent for loading lifeboats known as "The Birkenhead Drill"*

Ships are like women...
expensive to rig and difficult to steer.

Many a good sail makes a bad honeymoon.

Even the weakest river winds somewhere to the sea.

Better lose the anchor than the whole ship.

Help thy brother's boat across, and Lo!
Thine own has reached the shore.

A crisis is an opportunity riding the dangerous wind.

Learning is like rowing upstream;
not to advance is to drop back.

Everyone must row with the oars he has.

You have to go out. You don't have to come back.
—*U.S. Coast Guard motto*

It is not possible to step twice into the same river.

There is nothing that duct tape or roses can't fix.

Don't build a new boat out of old wood.

He knows the water best who has waded through it.

Fame like a river is narrowest at its source
and broadest afar off.

A man without money is like a ship without sails.

He that is embarked with the devil must sail with him.

Any port in a storm.

U.S.C.G.—Uncle Sam's Confused Group

I've spent most of my time
(sailing, boating, surfing, etc.),
The rest I've wasted.

Lighthouses don't ring bells and fire cannon to call
attention to their shining; they just shine on.

The mistakes of a learned man are like a shipwreck
which wrecks many others with it.

The best place to drink beer is at home.
Or on a river bank, if the fish don't bother you.

If you want to launch big ships,
you have to go where the water is deep.

Time and tide wait for no man.

A ship in harbor is safe,
but that's not why ships were built.

Give a man a fish and he'll eat for a day,
Teach him to fish and he'll keep bait in the fridge.

Nothing sucks. Atmospheric pressure pushes.

Do not have each foot on a different boat.

If you haven't run aground,
you haven't really been cruising.

For good food, good wine and for good fellowship
we thank God.

Drown not thyself to save a drowning man.

A sailor without a tattoo is like a ship without grog:
not seaworthy.

Rowing is the only sport that originated
as a form of capital punishment.

Here's looking at you dear!
Though I should pour a sea of wine,
My eyes would thirst for more.

Don't cross the river if you can't swim the tide.

He that is weather wise
Is seldom other wise.

No Quarter Given.
—*pirate toast*

It is good sailing with wind and tide.

Never test the depth of the water with both feet.

Heaven protects children, sailors and drunken men.

I'd rather be in the boat with a drink on the rocks,
Than in the drink with a boat on the rocks.

A collision at sea can ruin your entire day.

It's not the size of the board
But the length of the ride.
—*surfer wisdom*

It's not the size of the boat
But the motion of the ocean.

B.O.A.T — Break Out Another Thousand

The two happiest days of a boatowner's life:
the day he buys it and the day he sells it!

Here's to honor—get on her and stay on her!

Cruising costs as much as you have.

There is never any excuse
to put the comfort of the crew
above the safety of the vessel.

It is ill sailing against wind and tide.

Sailing is like standing fully clothed
under a cold shower tearing up twenty dollar bills.

For landlubbers that can't remember port
from starboard,
there is no more red port left!

You put the wind in my sails.

Sailors do it between the sheets.

Sailboat racing is not a matter of life and death—
it's much more serious than that.

Only sailors are blown offshore.

Rowers have the best strokes.

I'd rather be sailing.

Smooth seas do not make skillful sailors.

If it swells, ride it!
—*surfer axiom*

Man can't discover new oceans unless he has the
courage to lose sight of the shore.

Don't sail out further than you can row back.

Absent friends—though out of sight
we recognize them with our glasses.

Most of my money I spent on boats and women.
The rest I squandered!
or
I spent my money on wine, women and yachts—
the rest I wasted!

Big ships often sail on big debts.

If you're not living on the edge,
you're taking up too much space!

If you have to be somewhere by a certain date,
you aren't cruising, you're racing.

I sure hope my ship comes in before my dock rots.

Make not your sail too big for your ballast.

It takes a good storm to get the best out of a good sailor.

Without fear, there is no courage.
—*pirate toast*

While sailing on port tack an intersecting yacht called
"Starboard!"
I nonchalantly looked up, offered forth my wineglass
and invited "Port?"

True Virgins Make Dull Companions—Add Whiskey!
—*mnemonic device for converting true to magnetic compass*

The journey of a thousand miles begins with a broken
main halyard and a leaky toilet valve.

The Golden Rule:
Whoever has the gold makes the rules.
—*pirate toast*

Let him who knows not how to pray go to sea.

When my ship came in, I was at the airport.

The gods do not deduct from a man's allotted span,
those days spent sailing.

The gods do not deduct from man's allotted span the
hours spent in fishing.

The Immortal Memory of Admiral Lord Nelson.
—*October 21 is Trafalgar Day, when the toast is raised around the
world to Lord Admiral Nelson. This toast is taken in silence
(and with the left hand as Nelson lost his right arm at the
Battle of Santa Cruz de Tenerife).*

A boat stands firmer with two anchors.

My drinking team has a sailing problem!
—*t-shirt slogan*

May your joys be as deep as the ocean,
and your troubles as light as its foam.

May the bonds of friendship which tie our vessels
together continue to strengthen in the future.

To the great traditions of the U.S. Navy
and her many gallant leaders.

No one would ever have crossed the ocean if
he could have gotten off the ship in a storm.

Nautical Toasts

Exitio est avidum mare nautis
(The hungry sea is fatal to sailors)

There are four types of sailors:
Those who have been sea-sick;
and those who haven't yet;
Those who have run aground;
and those who haven't yet.

Sailors make money like horses and spend it like asses.

Approaching a dock with a boat is like
approaching a woman in a bar,
very seldom is a slow approach a poor approach.

Pray to God, but row for shore.

Raise your sail one foot, and you get ten feet of wind.

Adventure is never much fun while it's happening.

Fish, to taste right, must swim three times
—in water, in butter and in wine.

He was begotten in the galley and born under a gun.
Every hair was a rope yarn, every finger a fish-hook,
every tooth a marline-spike,
and his blood right good Stockholm tar.
—*navy epitaph*

A bad day of fishing is still better
than a good day at work.

Here lies the sailor Michael O'Day
Who died maintaining his right of way;
His course was clear, his will was strong,
But he's just as dead as if he'd been wrong.

Here's to four fishers bold;
Here's to the fish they caught,
Here's to the ones that got away,
And here's to the ones they bought.

If you didn't drink it, don't flush it.

There are two types of fisherman—
those who fish for sport and those who fish for fish.

Fishing is the sport of drowning worms.

There are only two absolute rules of thumb at sea:
Don't let the people in the water tank,
and don't let the water in the people tank.

A sailor must have his eye trained to the rocks and
sands as well as the north star.

When life's last sun goes feebly down
And death comes to our door,
When all the world's a dream to us,
We'll go to sea no more.

The three most useless things in a yacht are
a step ladder, a wheelbarrow and a naval officer.

For grog is our starboard, our larboard,
Our mainmast, our mizzen, our log—
At sea, or ashore, or when harbour'd,
The mariners compass is grog.
—*U.S. Navy song, early 19th century*

Underway is the only way.

"To their dignity, grace and style, but most of all tonight
we toast their courage... To those brave men."
"Hear! Hear!"
"To the stewards, the men who stoked the boilers, the
crew who shared that bravery as much as any man in a
tuxedo. . . . To those brave men."
"Hear! Hear!"
"To the young and old, the rich and the poor,
the ignorant and the learned, all who gave their lives
nobly to save women and children. To those brave men."
"Hear! Hear!"
"In these days of air disasters, death is sudden. . .
They had time to think and choose. . .
To those brave men."
"Hear! Hear!"
—*Tribute to the men of the RMS Titanic*

In Childhood's hour, with careless joy,
Upon the stream we glide;
With Youth's bright hopes we gaily speed
To reach the other side
Manhood looks forth with careful glance,
Time plies the steady oar,
While Old Age calmly waits to hear
the keel upon the shore.

The man doomed to sail
With the blast of the gale
Through billows Atlantic to steer
As he bends o'er the wave
Which may soon be his grave
Remembers his home with a tear.

When round the bowl the jovial crew
The early scenes of youth renew,
Tho' each his fav'rite fair will boast,
This is the universal toast,
May we, when toil and danger's o'er,
Cast anchor on our native shore.

How happy are we now the wind is abaft
And the boatswain he pipes, "Haul both our sheets aft,"
"Steady," says the Master, "It blows a fresh gale,
We'll soon reach our port, boys,
If the wind doth not fail."
Then drink about, Tom,
Although the ship roll,
We'll save our rich liquor
By slinging our bowl.

Navy Toasts

In Britain's Royal Navy, toasts were drunk at dinner to the reigning monarch (also known as the "Loyal Toast"). The navy was eventually accorded the privilege of remaining seated while drinking to the sovereign's health. The reason for this special permission is obscure in origin. Among the popular beliefs about this is that King Charles II, when on board the HMS *Royal Charles*, bumped his head on rising to reply to the toast.

In addition, traditional toasts were drunk on specific days of the week. They were:

Sunday – "Absent friends and those at sea."
Monday – "Our ships at sea."
Tuesday – "Our Men."
Wednesday – "Ourselves and no one like us."
Thursday – "A bloody war or a sickly season"
(and therefore more-rapid promotion).
A variant was "A bloody war and quick promotion."
Friday – "A willing foe and sea room."
Saturday – "Sweethearts and wives."
(someone would invariably pipe up "and may they never meet!")

In the U.S. Navy loyal toasting was practiced afloat and ashore until 1914, when alcohol was banned. The president was toasted instead of the king.

International Toasts

Here is a list of short toasts to get you through any international port of call. Their English equivalents are along the lines of "Cheers," "Bottoms Up," "To Your Health," and "Down the Hatch."

Afrikaans: *Gesondheid*
Albanian: *Shëndeti tuaj / Gezuar*
Arabic: *Fi sahitak*
Armenian: *Genatset*
Asturian: *Gayola*
Austrian: *Prost / Zum Wohl*
Azerbaijani: *Afiyæt olsun*
Bali: *Selemat*
Basque: *Topa*
Belgian: *Op uw gezonheid*
Bengali: *Joy*
Bosnian: *Zivjeli*
Brazilian: *Saude / Viva*
Breton: *Yec'hed mat*
Bulgarian: *Naz drave*
Catalan: *Salut*
Chinese: *Kong chien / Yum sen*
Cornish: *Yeghes da*
Creole: *Salud*
Croatian: *Zivjeli / U zdravlje*

Czech: *Na zdraví*
Danish: *Skål*
Dutch: *Proost*
Egyptian: *Fee sihetak*
Esperanto: *Sanon / Salutè*
Estonian: *Teie terviseks*
Farsi: *Ba'sal'a'ma'ti*
Finnish: *Kippis*
French: *À votre santé / Santé*
Frisian: *Tsjoch*
Galician: *Chinchín / Saúde*
German: *Prost, Auf ihr wohl*
Greek: *Gia'sou*
Greenlandic: *Kasugta*
Hawaiian: *Hipahipa / Okole maluna*
Hebrew: *Le'chaim (loc'hiem)*
Holooe: *Kam-poe*
Hungarian: *Egészségedre*
Icelandic: *Santanka nu / Skål*
Ido: *Ye vua saneso*
Indian: *Apki Lambi Umar Ke Liye*
Irish: *Sláinte*
Italian: *Salute / Cin cin*
Japanese: *Cumpai / Banzai*
Korean: *Konbe /Gombei*
Latin: *Sanitas bona / Bene tibi*
Latvian: *Prieka*
Lithuanian: *I sveikata*

Malaysian: *Minum*
Mandarin: *Gan bei*
Maori: *Kia ora*
Mexican: *Salud*
Moroccan: *Saha wa'afiab*
Norwegian: *Skål*
Occitan: *A la vòstra*
Pakistani: *Sanda bashi*
Philippine: *Mabuhay*
Polish: *Na zdrowie / Sto lat*
Portuguese: *Saúde*
Rumanian: *Noroc*
Russian: *Na zdorovie*
Serbian: *Zivjeli / U zdravlje*
Sesotho: *Nqa*
Slovak: *Na zdravie*
Slovenian: *Na zdravje*
Spanish: *Salud*
Swahili: *Afya / Vifijo*
Swedish: *Skål*
Tagalog: *Mabuhay*
Thai: *Chook-die / Sawasdi*
Turkish: *Serefe*
Ukrainian: *Na zdorov'ya*
Welsh: *Llechyd da / Hwyll*
Yiddish: *Lechaim*
Yugoslavian: *Ziveo / Ziveli*
Zulu: *Oogy wawa*

The Gin Pennant was often followed with the flags Romeo, Papa, and Charlie for "Request the Pleasure of your Company."

Potable Quotables

"Only fools and passengers drink at sea."
—*Allan Villiers*

"I never knew a sailor, in my life,
who would not prefer a pot of hot coffee
or chocolate, on a cold night, to all the rum afloat."
—*Richard Henry Dana*

"The cure for anything is salt water
—sweat, tears of the sea."
—*Isak Dineson*

"I've drank to your health with others,
I've drank to your health alone.
I've drank to your health so many times,
That I've almost ruined my own."
—*Attributed to Admiral William F. "Bull" Halsey*

"You don't get sea stories by buying sailors beer."
—*Allan Villiers*

"Drinking is a way of ending the day."
—*Ernest Hemingway*

"For all at last return to the sea
—to Oceanus, the ocean river,
Like the ever-flowing stream of time,
the beginning and the end."
—*Rachel Carson*

"Any damn fool can circumnavigate the world sober.
It takes a really good sailor to do it drunk."
—*Sir Francis Chichester, while loading his boat with gin*

"Tell that to the Marines—the sailor's won't believe it."
—*Sir Walter Scott*, Redgauntlet

"Don't talk to me about naval tradition.
It's nothing but rum, sodomy and the lash."
—*Winston Churchill*

"Bacchus has drowned more men than Neptune."
—*Giuseppe Garibaldi*

"Wine hath drowned more men than the sea."
—*Robert Fuller*

"No matter how long the river,
the river will reach the sea."
—*Eugene Fitch Ware*

"You and I were a couple of drunks on a sea of booze
and the boat sank."
—*Jack Lemmon*, Days of Wine and Roses

"To the wonder and mystery of the ships,
And the magic of the sea."
—*Henry Wadsworth Longfellow*, "My Lost Youth"

"The sea hates a coward."
—*Eugene O'Neill*

"I believe that this would be a good time for a beer!"
President Franklin D. Roosevelt
upon ratification of the 21st Amendment, repealing Prohibition

"Thought is the wind and knowledge is the sail."
—*David Hare*

"If all else fails, immortality can always be assured
by spectacular error."
—*John Kenneth Galbraith*

"Ships and seamen rot in harbor."
—*Horatio Nelson*

"Any man who may be asked what he did to make his
life worthwhile can respond with a good deal
of pride and satisfaction,
'I served in the United States Navy'"
—*President John F. Kennedy, 1963*

"Water is the only drink for a wise man."
—*Henry David Thoreau*

"We may have all come on different ships,
but we're all in the same boat now."
—*Martin Luther King, Jr.*

"You can't drown yourself in drink,
I've tried, you float."
—*John Barrymore*

"Fishing is much more than fish…
It is the great occasion when we
may return to the fine simplicity of our forefathers."
—*Herbert Hoover*

"My boat is on the shore, And my bark is on the sea:
But, before I go, Tom Moore,
Here's a double health to thee!"
—*Lord Byron*

"We few, we happy few, we band of brothers;
For he today that sheds his blood with me
shall be my brother."
—*William Shakespeare*, Henry V

"It is part of a sailor's life to die well."
—*Stephen Decatur*

"At sea a fellow comes out.
Saltwater is like wine in that respect."
—*Herman Melville*

"Damn the torpedoes! Full speed ahead!"
—*David Glasgow Farragut*

"There is nothing—absolutely nothing—half so much
worth doing as simply messing about in boats."
—*Kenneth Grahame*, Wind in the Willows

"To long lives and short wars!"
—*Colonel Sherman Potter, "M*A*S*H"*

"The larger the island of knowledge,
the longer the shoreline of wonder."
—*Ralph W. Sockman*

When one has good wine,
A graceful junk,
And a maiden's love,
Why envy the immortal gods?
—*Li Po*

"From one s.o.b. to another."
—*George C. Scott as General George Patton while linking arms
with a Russian Field Marshall in the
1970 Academy Award-winning film* Patton.

"The art of the sailor is to leave nothing to chance."
—*Annie Van De Wiele*

"The winds and waves are always on the side
of the ablest navigators."
—*Edward Gibbon*

"It was involuntary. They sank my boat."
—*John F. Kennedy's reply when asked how he became a war hero.*

"I like terra firma—the more firma, the less terra."
—*George S. Kaufman*

"Ships are the nearest thing to dreams
that hands have ever made."
—*Robert N. Rose*

"America and England:
and may they never have any division
but the Atlantic between them."
—*Charles Dickens*

"Man your ships and may the force be with you."
—*from the film* Star Wars

"If fishes were wishes
the ocean would be all of our desire."
—*Gertrude Stein*

"Does anybody want any flotsam, I've gotsam?
Does anybody want any jetsam? I can getsam."
—*Ogden Nash*

"At sea, every dawn is a thrill."
—*Nicholas Monsarrat*

"Whiskey drowns some troubles and floats a lot more."
—*Robert C. Edwards*

"A ship is like a lady's watch, always out of repair."
—*Richard Henry Dana*

"People are like water and the ruler a boat.
Water can support a boat or overturn it."
—*Li Shimim*

"Don't worry about the world coming to an end today.
It's already tomorrow in Australia."
—*Charles Schulz*

"Land was created to provide a place for boats to visit."
—*Brooks Atkinson*

"Not all who wander are lost."
—*JRR Tolkien*

"Home is the sailor, home from the sea."
—*Robert Louis Stevenson*

"One flag, one land, one heart,
one hand, one nation evermore."
—*Oliver Wendell Holmes*

"The ocean is a body of water occupying about two-thirds of a world made for man—who has no gills."
—*Ambrose Bierce*

"Boats, automobiles, and liquor all have their thrills,
but either they do not last long
or they cost a lot to keep up."
—*L. Francis Herreshoff*

"Never worry about stepping on anyone's toes.
People who get their toes stepped on are standing still
or sitting down on the job."
—*Admiral Arleigh Burke*

"Thank God I have done my duty."
—*Admiral Horatio Nelson's last words*

"Nothing ever tasted any better than a cold beer on a
beautiful afternoon with nothing to look forward to
but more of the same."
—*Hugh Hood*

"Anchors Aweigh, my boys, Anchors Aweigh.
Farewell to college joys, we sail at break of day-ay-ay-ay.
Through our last night on shore, drink to the foam,
Until we meet once more.
Here's wishing you a happy voyage home."
—*Anchor's Aweigh, unofficial U.S. Navy service song*

"Which shall it be: bankruptcy of purse
or bankruptcy of life?"
—*Sterling Hayden,* Wanderer

"Country:
To her we drink, for her we pray,
Our voices silent never;
For her we'll fight, come what may,
The stars and stripes forever!"
—*Stephen Decatur*

"Rowing harder doesn't help if the boat is headed
in the wrong direction."
—*Kenichi Ohmae*

"To the question, 'When were your spirits at their
lowest ebb?' the obvious answer seemed to be,
'When the gin gave out.'"
—*Sir Francis Chichester*

"Shiver My Timbers
Said Captain Mack
We're Ten Knots Out
But We're Turning back
I Forgot My
Burma Shave"
—*Burma Shave Sign*

"The snotgreen sea. The scrotumtightening sea."
—*James Joyce*, Ulysses

"Only two sailors, in my experience, never ran aground.
One never left port and the other was an atrocious liar."
—*Don Bamford*

"After a ship has tried alcohol once,
it takes to water for the rest of its life."
—*Franklin Delano Roosevelt, Assistant Secretary of the U.S. Navy,
when asked why the Navy continued to christen ships
with alcohol during Prohibition.*

"Don't Give up the Ship!"
—*Captain James Lawrence*

"Faith is the soul riding at anchor."
—*H.W. Shaw*

"We should not moor a ship with one anchor,
or our life with one hope."
—*Epictetus*

"A reformer is a man who rides through a sewer
in a glass-bottomed boat."
—*James J. Walker*

"A good navy is not a provocation to war.
It is the surest guaranty of peace."
—*President Theodore Roosevelt, 1902*

"Whoever can hold the sea
has command of everything."
—*Themistocles*

"Now - bring me that horizon."
—*Final line in the film* Pirates of the Caribbean

"I wish to have no connection with any ship that
does not sail fast for I intend to go in harm's way."
—*Captain John Paul Jones, 1778*

"You can't stop the waves, but you can learn to surf."
—*Jon Kabat-Zinn*

"At sea, I learned how little a person needs,
not how much."
—*Robin Lee Graham*

"A ship may belong to her captain,
but lifeboats belong to the crew."
—*John Farrow*

"A man without a woman is like a ship without a sail
Is like a boat without a rudder, or a shirt without a tail
Now a man without a woman is like a wreck upon the sand
But if there is one thing worse in this universe
Then it's a woman, I said a woman
I mean a woman without a man."
—*Alfred Williams*

"Uncommon valor was a common virtue."
—*Fleet Admiral Chester W. Nimitz*
on U.S. forces at the battle of Iwo Jima, 1945

"Claret is the liquor for boys; port for men;
but he who aspires to be a hero must drink brandy."
—*Samuel Johnson*

"Wind is to us what money is to life on shore."
—*Sterling Hayden*

"The only way to get a good crew is to marry one."
—*Eric Hiscock*

"I entertained on a cruising trip that was so much fun that I had to sink my yacht to make my guests go home."
—*F. Scott Fitzgerald*

"I must go down to the sea again,
to the lonely sea and sky,
And all I ask is a tall ship
and a star to steer her by."
—*John Masefield*, "Sea Fever"

"It isn't that life ashore is distasteful to me.
But life at sea is better."
—*Sir Francis Drake*

"We have met the enemy and they are ours."
—*Oliver Hazard Perry*

"Bad cooking is responsible for more trouble at sea than all other things put together."
—*Thomas Fleming Day*

"When crew and captain understand each other to the core
It takes a gale and more than a gale to put their ship ashore."
—*Rudyard Kipling*

"I want a boat that drinks six, eats four and sleeps two."
—*Ernest K. Gann*

"Boats, like whiskey, are all good."
—*R.D. "Pete" Culler*

"Wine is bottled poetry."
—*Robert Louis Stevenson*

"The sea is a great university of the story-telling art."
—*Norman Freeman*

"Why don't you slip out of those wet clothes
and into a dry Martini."
—*Robert Benchley*

"People who drink to drown their sorrows should be
told that sorrow knows how to swim."
—*Ann Landers*

"For we could not now take time for further search
(to land our ship) our victuals being much spent,
especially our Beere."
—*Ship's log of the Mayflower*

"I really don't know why it is that all of us are so
committed to the sea, except I think it's because in
addition to the fact that the sea changes, and the light
changes, and ships change, it's because we all came
from the sea. All of us have in our veins the exact
same percentage of salt in our blood that exists in the
ocean, and therefore we have salt in our blood sweat
and tears. We are tied to the ocean. And when we go
back to the sea—whether it is to sail or to watch it—
we are going back from whence we came."
—*President John F. Kennedy*
at a 1962 dinner celebrating the America's Cup.

"Without a respectable navy—alas America!"
—*John Paul Jones*

"He is the best sailor who can steer
within the fewest points of the wind, and exact a
motive power out of the greatest obstacles."
—*Henry David Thoreau*

"One ship sails east and another sails west
With the self-same winds that blow.
Tis the set of the sail and not the gale
Which determines the way they go.
As the winds of the sea are the ways of fate
As we voyage along through life,
Tis the act of the soul that determines the goal,
And not the calm or the strife."
—*Ella Wheeler Wilcox*

"Sobriety brought a man under suspicion."
—*Daniel Defoe, writing about pirates in New Providence*

"Anyone can hold the helm when the sea is calm."
—*Syrus Pubilius*

"When you put to sea in your own boat,
you become a different and,
for the time being at least, a better man."
—*James S. Pritkin*

"Payday came and with it beer."
—*Rudyard Kipling*

"Find a way, or make a way."
—*Admiral Robert E. Peary*

"Our country! In her intercourse with foreign nations,
may she always be in the right;
but our country right or wrong."
—*Stephen Decatur*

"*In vino veritas.*"
(In wine there is truth)
—*Pliny the Elder*

"If one does not know to which port one is sailing,
no wind is favorable."
—*Seneca (the Younger)*

"Love one another, but make not a bond of love;
Let it rather be a moving sea
between the shores of your souls."
—*Kahlil Gibran*

"Better sleep with a sober cannibal
than a drunk Christian."
—*Herman Melville*, Moby Dick

"Good evening Mr. and Mrs. America
and all the ships at sea."
—*Walter Winchell's famous radio salutation*

"It is hard to describe the fascination of the sea as to explain the beauty of a woman, for, to each man, either it is self-evident, or no argument can help him see it."
—*Claud Worth*

"Oh was there ever a sailor free to choose, that didn't settle, somewhere near the sea."
—*Rudyard Kipling*

"He who will not be ruled by the rudder, must be ruled by the rock."
—*Isaac D'Israeli*

"Here's to fishing—a grand delusion enthusiastically promoted by liars in old clothes."
—*Don Marquis*

"for whatever we lose (like a you or a me) it's always ourselves we find in the sea."
—*e. e. cummings*

"The sea doth wash away all human ills."
—*Euripideas, quoted by Plato when cured of an illness in Egypt by the use of seawater.*

"Twenty years from now you will be more disappointed in the things that you didn't do than in the ones you did do. So throw off the bow lines. Sail away from the safe harbor. Catch the trade winds in your sails. Explore. Dream. Discover."
—*Mark Twain*

"The water was not fit to drink. To make it palatable, we had to add whiskey. By diligent effort, I learned to like it."
—*Winston Churchill*

"They that go down to the sea in ships, that do business in great waters, these see the works of the Lord and his wonders in the deep."
—*Bible, Psalms 107:23–24*

"Fishing is a discipline in the equality of men— for all men are equal before fish."
—*Herbert Hoover*

"It has always been my private conviction that any man who pits his intelligence against a fish and loses has it coming."
—*John Steinbeck*

"Full fathom five thy father lies;
Of his bones are coral made;
Those are pearls that were his eyes;
Nothing of him that does fade,
But doth suffer a sea-change
Into something rich and strange.
Sea-nymphs hourly ring his knell:
Ding-dong,
Hark! Now I hear them – Ding-dong, bell."
—*William Shakespeare*, "The Tempest"

"Never interrupt your enemy
when he is making a mistake."
—*Napoleon Bonaparte*

"Rocked in the cradle of the deep
I lay me down in peace to sleep
Secure I rest upon a wave
For Thou, O Lord! Hast power to save."
—*Emma Hart Willard, written at sea 1831*

"The course of life is like the sea;
Men come and go; tides rise and fall;
And that is all of history."
—*Joaquin Miller*

"Here's looking at you, kid."
—*Humphrey Bogart to Ingrid Bergman in "Casablanca"**
*(OK Casablanca *is not a nautical movie, but Humphrey Bogart did
star in perhaps three of the greatest maritime films of all time—*
The African Queen, The Caine Mutiny *and*
Action in the North Atlantic.)

"There is a tide in the affairs of men,
Which, taken at the flood, leads on to fortune;
Omitted, all the voyages of their life
Is bound in shallows and in miseries.
On such a full sea are we now afloat;
And we must take the current when it serves,
Or lose our ventures."
—*William Shakespeare*

"We all like to see people seasick
when we are not ourselves."
—*Mark Twain*, Innocents Abroad

"There are more fish taken out of a stream
than were ever in it."
—*Oliver Herford*

"On land I am a hero. At sea I am a coward."
—*Adolf Hitler*

"All the rivers run into the sea; yet the sea is not full;
unto the place from whence the rivers come,
thither they return again."
—*The Bible, Ecclesiastes* 1:6

"The sea was so much in love with him
that she wanted to keep him for her alone ..."
—*Pascal Gelebart-Begue*
on the death of French sailor Eric Tabarly

"Water, not necessary to life but rather life itself,
thou fillest us with a gratification that exceeds the
delight of the senses."
—*Antoine de Saint-Exupery*

"Faintly as tolls the evening chime,
Our voices keep tune and our oars keep time."
—*Thomas Moore*

"Many men go fishing all of their lives without
knowing that it is not fish they are after."
—*Henry David Thoreau*

"Money can't buy you happiness. But it can buy you a
yacht big enough to pull up right alongside it."
—*David Lee Roth*

"I joined the navy to see the world;
And what did we see?
We saw the sea."
—*Irving Berlin*

"If people concentrated on the really important
things in life, there'd be a shortage of fishing poles."
—*Doug Larson*

"No man will be a sailor who has contrivance enough
to get himself into jail; for being in a ship is being in a
jail, with the chance of being drowned."
—*Samuel Johnson*

"As idle as a painted ship
Upon a painted ocean."
—*Samuel Taylor Coleridge*, "Rime of the Ancient Mariner"

"Give a man a fish and he has food for a day;
teach him how to fish and you can get rid of him for
the entire weekend."
—*Zenna Schaffer*

"Blood is thicker than water!"
—*Commodore Josiah Tattnail, U.S.Navy*

"It's easy to grin
When your ship's come in
And you've got the stock market beat,
But a man worth while
is the man who can smile
when his pants are too tight in the seat."
—*Judge Smails in the film* Caddyshack

"There's a fine line between fishing
and just standing on the shore like an idiot."
—*Steven Wright*

"Them that dies'll be the lucky ones."
—*Long John Silver,* Treasure Island

"The charm of fishing is that it is the pursuit of what
is elusive but attainable,
a perpetual series of occasions for hope."
—*John Buchan*

"A woman should never be seen eating or drinking,
unless it be lobster salad and Champagne, the only
true feminine and becoming viands."
—*Lord Byron*

"Vessels large may venture more,
But little boats should keep near shore."
—*Benjamin Franklin*

"Everybody in life gets the same amount of ice.
The rich get it in the summer and the poor in the winter."
—*Words found in the typewriter of sportswriter
Bat Masterson after he suffered a fatal heart attack*

"Between the dream and the deed lie the doldrums."
—*Herb Payson*

"Liquor contains considerable energy, but its function
in an open boat is to sustain morale during night
watches and in cold and squally weather."
—How to Abandon Ship *by Phil Richards and John J. Banigan,
Cornell Maritime Press, 1942*

"Oh, we don't give a damn for our old Uncle Sam
Way-o, whisky and gin!
Lend us a hand when we stand in to land
Just give us time to run the rum in."
—*The Smugglers' Chantey, Joseph Chase Allen, 1921*

"A ship is always referred to as 'she' because it costs so much to keep one in paint and powder."
—*attributed to Admiral Chester W. Nimitz*

"Heave Ho, My Lads, Heave Ho
It's a Long, Long pull with our hatches full,
Bravings the wind, braving the sea,
Fighting the treacherous foe.
Heave Ho, My Lads, Heave Ho
Let the Sea Roll High or low
We can cross any ocean, sail any river
Give us the goods and we'll deliver
Damn the submarines
We are the men of the merchant marines."
—*U.S. Merchant Marine Anthem*

"A Human Being should be able to change a diaper, plan an invasion, butcher a hog, conn a ship, design a building, write a sonnet, balance accounts, build a wall, set a bone, comfort the dying, take orders, give orders, cooperate, act alone, solve equations, analyze a new problem, pitch manure, program a computer, cook a tasty meal, fight efficiently and die gallantly. Specialization is for insects."
—*Robert Heinlein*

"There is nothing more enticing, disenchanting, and
enslaving than life at sea."
—*Joseph Conrad*

"I only regret that I have but one life
to lose for my country."
—*Nathan Hale*

"It's five o'clock somewhere."
—*Alan Jackson/ Jimmy Buffett*

When the beer flag is flown upside down it indicates that the
cooler has gone dry and a serious situation exists on board.

Fun Facts &
Amusing Anecdotes

The relationship between alcohol and the sea is evidenced in so many ways—a body of water is often referred to as "the drink;" boaters, going below, retreat to the saloon; and, ships not christened with alcohol are deemed unseaworthy. Over the years this bond has given rise to thousands of humorous stories and amusing anecdotes. Here are just a few:

• Franklin Delano Roosevelt, who, while serving as Secretary of the Navy, was approached by a member of the Women's Temperance Union who complained to him about the sin of christening ships with champagne. Roosevelt replied, "Madam, remember: After a ship has tried alcohol once, it takes to water for the rest of its life."

• The word booze was thought to have been brought into everyday language by sailors, from the Dutch, *buizen*, meaning to drink to excess.

• "Bar - Long, low-lying navigational hazard, usually awash, found at river mouths and harbor entrances, where it is composed of sand and mud, and shore, where it is made of mahogany or some other dark wood. Sailors can be found in large numbers around both." (Source: *Sailing: A Dictionary for Landlubbers, Old Salts, & Armchair Drifters* by Henry Beard and Roy McKie (Workman Publishing 1981)—still the funniest book of its kind).

• Blackbeard the pirate is said to have drank rum and gunpowder.

• Pimm's and lemonade (also called Classic Pimm's), drunk in pints, is a traditional beverage for rowing regattas, including Britain's Henley Royal Regatta, competed every first weekend in July on the river Thames. Pimm's, a gin-based liquor made in England, was created in 1859 by English oyster bar owner James Pimm. The recipe, it is said, is a secret known to only six persons.

• The French submersible *Nautile* raised bottles of Bass Ale from the wreck of the RMS *Titanic* in 1996.

• Navy etiquette suggests a no treating rule. One is advised not to offer to buy a drink at the bar as it may embarrass another who may not be able to return the compliment.

• When Benjamin Franklin was American emissary to

France, the British ambassador led off with a toast to his king: "George III, who, like the sun in its meridian, spreads lustre throughout and enlightens the world." Not to be outdone, the French minister said: "To the illustrious Louis XVI, who, like the moon, sheds his mild and benevolent rays on and influences the globe." Finally, Franklin rose and responded: "To George Washington, commander of the American armies, who, like Joshua of old, commanded the sun and moon to stand still, and both obeyed."

• French explorer Jean-Baptiste Charcot (1867-1936) made many important discoveries and surveyed many miles of the Antarctic coastline aboard his vessel *Pourquois-Pas?* ("Why Not"). The vessel was known for carrying the finest stock of wines ever taken to the polar regions.

• Sir Ernest Shackleton's newspaper ad for his 1914 expedition to the South Pole read as such: "Men Wanted For Hazardous Journey, small wages, bitter cold, long months of darkness, constant danger, safe return doubtful. Honour and recognition in case of success." People had to have been drinking to have volunteered.

• Sir Francis Chichester was 65 years old when he embarked on his voyage around the world. Alone, on his 53-foot ketch *Gypsy Moth IV*, he completed the trip in 262 days. Starting from Plymouth Harbor in England, he headed south, logging-in a 14,000-mile nonstop passage to Sydney, Australia. When asked the question, "When were your spirits at their lowest ebb?" put to him during a press conference in Sydney, he replied, "When the gin gave out."

• On January 28, 1970 the "Great Rum Debate" took place in the Britain's House of Commons, and July 30, 1970 was "Black Tot Day," when the last pipe of "Up Spirits" was sounded in the Royal Navy.

> *"Fifteen men on a dead man's chest*
> *Yo ho ho and a bottle of rum*
> *Drink and the devil had done for the rest"*

• Robert Louis Stevenson came across the reference to Dead Man's Chest in an old text and used it in his 1883 work *Treasure Island*. Dead Man's Chest is a tiny isle that forms part of the British Virgin Islands in the Caribbean Sea. Folklore claims that pirate Edward Teach, known as Blackbeard, punished a mutinous crew by marooning them on Dead Man's Chest, which has high cliffs and no water and is inhabited by pelicans and snakes. Each sailor was given a cutlass and a bottle of rum. Teach's hope was that the pirates would kill each other, but when he returned after a month he found 15 men had survived.

• The fledgling U.S. Navy was modeled along the lines of Britain's Royal Navy and, early in 1794 the Congress enacted into law that a daily ration for American sailors would be "one half pint of distilled spirits," or in lieu thereof, "one quart of beer."

• A mnemonic for the decimal expansion of π (3.14159265358979323846264) can be made into a drinking phrase. Each successive digit is the number of letters in the corresponding word: "How I want a drink, alcoholic of course, after the heavy lectures involving quantum mechanics. All of the geometry. Herr Planck is fairly hard."

• According to legend, John Jacob Astor IV was standing at the bar when the RMS *Titanic* collided with an iceberg and began to sink. "I asked for ice," he is said to have to declared, "but this is ridiculous!"

• On his way to winning three Bermuda Races in the 1950s, yachtsman Carlton Mitchell wrote, "dinner was served with wine in the saloon of *Finisterre*."

• The first U.S. Navy vessel to be christened was the USS *Constitution*. While water was used to christen the ship, *Constitution* refused to budge from her perch on the slipway. As lore has it, someone produced a bottle of Madeira, smashed it against the bow, and the ship slid gracefully into the river.

• The first U.S. Navy ship to be christened with champagne was also the navy's first steel battleship. The USS *Maine* was christened in a ceremony on November 18, 1890 at the New York Navy Yard. Unfortunately the *Maine* suffered a fate not unlike the champagne bottle that christened her.

• In 1990 the traditional bottle of champagne was put aside and replaced by a bottle containing a blend of eight Kentucky Bourbons to christen the Trident submarine USS *Kentucky*.

• When Prohibition was repealed in 1933 the thirty-plus flag officers of the U.S. Navy unanimously turned down President Franklin Delano Roosevelt's offer to reinstate the wine mess aboard, which had been abolished by Navy Secretary Josephus Daniels in 1914.

• Many boaters believe it custom to appease the gods when opening a new bottle of liquor on board. They spray offering to the wind gods, pour a shot over the side for King Neptune, and spill a little on deck to re-christen the vessel.

• *Stars and Stripes*, the yacht that won the 1988 America's Cup was christened using a bottle of break-away glass—the same material used to make the windows that stuntmen jump through and beer bottles they break for bar scenes. To replicate the proper foam, drops of dish washing soap were added.

• *The Love Boat* craze of the 1970 launched a drinking game in reruns. Before the show starts, each player chooses what character s/he will play. During the show, when ever the character appears on screen, the player must drink for the duration of the appearance. If the character is simply referred to without being present, one drink must be taken.

• Rum runner Bill McCoy was one of the most celebrated characters of the Prohibition era. He set a standard that the liquor he carried be the best available... "The Real McCoy."

• Many skippers of old considered it unlucky for a ship to get underway without the crew first roistering ashore and all coming aboard drunk.

• Sinbad, the canine mascot of the Coast Guard cutter *Campbell* during World War II, was well-known in over one-hundred world ports for his ability to consume beer.

• In the late eighteenth-century the British Parliament decreed that each sailor must drink a pint of lime juice daily as a preventative to scurvy, thus came the nickname of "Limey" for British ships and Britishers in general.

• Water is removed from the table before toasts are proposed in the Royal Navy. This stems from the late seventeenth-century when England had two Kings, one, James II, a Catholic, was "over the water" in France, and toasting him was considered a treasonous act.

• In the old navy, when sailors returned from liberty they were marked in the logbook as either "CS," meaning clean and sober, or "DD," which stood for drunk and dirty.

• On November 13, 1968, the Beatles' animated classic *Yellow Submarine* premiered in the U.S. It later became a cocktail: $1^{1}/_{2}$ oz. Rum, 1 oz. Orange Curacao, Splash of Sour mix. Shake with ice and pour into a highball glass.

• German sailors offer the toast "*besanchot an*," which literally means "the mainsail is set,"—the equivalent of "splice the main brace."

• The unique taste of Line Aquavit is obtained by preserving it in oak barrels in the hold of Norwegian Shipping Line's ships. The liqueur crosses the Equator twice and is shaken in rough seas and subjected to extreme change of temperature before being bottled. The drink is often enjoyed by adding clam juice, which surely makes it the most nautical of all drinks.

Glossary of "Booze on Board"

In the early days of ocean sailing, alcoholic beverages were carried to supplement water. Water would quickly develop algae and slime in wooden barrels while wine and spirits could remain drinkable for months.

Thus began the strong bond between the sailor and spirits. For example, on an eighteenth-century Royal Navy man-of-war daily rations for seamen included eight pints of beer. Over the centuries alcohol became a form of relief for sailors, both afloat and ashore, and, later, the rum ration became a means of controlling seamen. Drunkenness became synonymous with sailors and the sea.

Whether for diversion, for dependency or for discipline, traditions, toasts, songs and slang evolved. And as so much of our culture and language is anchored in the sea, many of the words, phrases and expressions that sailors coined for drink and drinking have entered into our everyday speech. Following is a lexicon of phrases, drinking terms and idioms blended with alcohol icons that have a nautical significance.

Bilgewater - colloquial term for tasteless beer. Oddly enough, many sailors will leave a few beers in the bilge to chill down. One story has it that a sailor was doing just that aboard his steel ketch when it was struck by lightning, welding the cans of beer to the inside of the hull.

Binge - old mariner's term for rinsing or cleaning out a cask. A sailor who had "cleaned out" a cask of rum was said to have gone on a binge.

Black Tot Day - July 31, 1970, when the rum ration was abolished in Britain's Royal Navy, ending more than 300 years of tradition.

Blessing of the Fleet - a centuries-old tradition originating in southern European, predominantly Catholic, fishing communities, where the blessing of boats by a local priest was meant to ensure a safe and bountiful season. Such celebrations were usually accompanied by merriment and prodigious amounts of alcohol—especially red wine.

Bloody Mary - the classic pick-me-up (and perfect hair of the "sea dog") that, as legend has it, was first called the "Red Snapper." The drink was first mixed in the 1920s in Harry's bar in Paris. *Apium graveolens* (a.k.a. celery), *de rigueur* with a Bloody, was once believed to be a tonic for alcoholism.

Boat drink - a colorful drink, usually made with fruit, that is drunk on a boat, near a boat, or while wishing one was on a boat. Quaffing these concoctions was certainly made more popular by the Jimmy Buffett song "Boat Drinks."

Christening - ceremony for when a ship is launched. It is traditional to christen a ship by breaking a bottle of alcohol across its prow. Wine, long the traditional liquid used to christen a ship, was replaced at the close of the 19th century. Champagne became the popular liquid with which to christen a ship because of its image as the aristocrat of wines and the fact that its contents under pressure would inject a new dimension to the ceremony. (BTW, 60 degrees F. is the ideal temperature for breaking a bottle of champagne as it is thought to provide the most spray and foam.)

Cocktail/ Beer pennant/ flag - flag showing a wine/ martini glass or beer mug flown to let other boaters know that drinks are afloat. It is the modern equivalent of the gin pennant

Cuba Libre or Rum & Cola - during the Spanish-American War in the late 1800s American soldiers took Coca-Cola, a new soft drink at the time, with them in the fight for Cuban independence. At that time a new drink was created—the "Cuba Libre," the freedom of Cuba drink, which consisted of Coca-Cola, rum, and a lime wedge. Today there are numerous variations on the theme.

Cup of Joe - sailor slang for a mug of coffee so named for Josephus Daniels who, while U.S. Secretary of the Navy, did away with the alcohol aboard U.S. Navy ships. Since then the strongest beverage aboard was coffee, or a "cup of Joe." Coffee became the drink of choice aboard U.S. ships as a result of King George III's instituting a tax on tea and retaliation by colonists in the famous Boston Tea Party in 1773. The Continental Congress declared coffee the national drink of the colonies and aboard U.S. Navy ships and American sailors promptly switched from tea to coffee.

Daiquiri - rum concoction that is considered the drink of the West Indies. Made of rum, lime juice and sugar, it takes its name from the village of Daiquiri near Santiago, Cuba, where the cocktail originated around 1900. It was named either by American engineers working there, or by the U.S. troops who arrived there in 1898.

Dark & Stormy - Bermuda's national drink and yes, you do need the proper ingredients. Gosling's Black Seal Rum and Barritts Bermuda Ginger Beer (it must be Barritts). Squeeze a lemon wedge around the rim of the glass and garnish. Supposedly the rum improves your disposition and the ginger beer keeps your stomach settled. Post a lookout because these can overtake you with little warning. If the Gosling's out-lasts the ginger beer, here are a few other options: Gosling's Black Seal Rum on the rocks (lime optional), aka "Gosling's Hard Aground;" Gosling's Black Seal Rum, chilled, neat, with fresh squeezed lime juice, often called a "Scurvy Shot;" Gosling's Black Seal Rum in coffee (any way one likes coffee), called a "Goodnight Cap;" and Gosling's Black Seal Rum and Cola... well, that's just a waste of good rum!

Dead Soldier - an empty bottle of wine, spirit or beer. Originally the expression was "dead marine," believed coined by Britain's William IV, known as the "Sailor King." While aboard ship he ordered the steward to remove the "dead marines" to make room for new bottles.

Dining-In - a formal feast to honor military victories and individual achievements. Today it is largely a mili-tary ceremony with established protocol that includes a dinner and toasts honoring the feats of individuals and organizations.

Dressing Ship - practice of rigging signal flags aboard a vessel to commemorate a special date or occasion. Invitations are often sent to enlist help and the event is usually viewed as an occasion to crack open a few bev-erages. The sequence recommended to dress ship with a harmonious color pattern throughout is, starting from forward: AB2, UJ1, KE3, GH6, IV5, FL4, DM7, PO Third Repeater, RN First Repeater, ST Zero, CX9, WQ8, ZY Second Repeater.

Dutch Courage - known today as "liquid courage" it is said to derive from Dutch practice of drinking before battle in the maritime wars between Britain and Holland.

Gin & Tonic - the Brits developed this drink for ice-less "colonial" environments (gin was to Her Majesty's Army what rum was to the Royal Navy). Tonic water was invented to disguise the unpleasant taste of the medicinal quinine (necessary to fight malaria in the tropics). Tonic combined well with gin and the "Golf November Tango" was born. GNT made the leap from shore and today it has become de rigueur for on-board entertaining. As for tonic, give it some "Schweppervescence!" in honor of Commander Whitehead, the refined bearded seafaring gent who pushed Schweppes Tonic Water in ads back in the 1950s and 60s. Add plenty of lime to ward off any onset of scurvy, and if you're out of ice, just drop some nuts and bolts in the drink and occasionally shake it up for the ice-like clinking sound!

Gin Pennant - flag signal, first flown by the Royal Navy, that is an invitation to others to row over and enjoy a tipple. The pennant was originally the opposite of today's starboard pennant—the green and white reversed. (Other variations have been the starboard pennant with a wine or cocktail glass.) It was often followed with the flags Romeo, Papa, and Charlie for "Request the Pleasure of your Company." Modern-day usage is the cocktail pennant or beer pennant. When flown upside down it indicates that the martini shaker or cooler has gone dry and a serious situation exists on board.

Grog - rum diluted with water. Brandy was part of a sailor's daily rations in the Royal Navy until the conquest of Jamaica in 1687 when rum replaced it. In 1740, Admiral Vernon decided his fleet got a little too much rum and issued an order to have the daily ration of one pint of rum diluted with water. Since Vernon's nickname was "Old Grogram" because of the material out of which his boat cloak was made, the watered down rum immediately became known as "grog." Later, lemon was added to grog to fight scurvy and by 1850 lime was more commonly used. "Groggy" is what happened to you when you over-indulged in it. Interestingly enough, Mount Vernon, George Washington's home, was named after "Old Grogram" by Lawrence Washington

(Washington's brother) after having served with him during the War of Jenkins Ear.

Grog Blossom - the enlarged red nose of an alcoholic.

Grogshop - sailor terms for a shop or room where strong liquors are sold and/or drunk.

"Half Seas Over" - a person so inebriated as to be incapable of steering a steady course. It comes from the description of a ship run aground on a reef or rock with seas breaking over her.

Hawse (to freshen the hawse) - the drinking of spirits to revive oneself after time on deck in inclement weather.

Head - sailor's term for a bathroom (a place frequented after a few drinks). The term comes from the place where the crew relieved themselves—all the way forward on the ship near the figurehead.

Hot Rum Toddy - rum mixed with hot water, brown sugar, a dash of cinnamon and a dollop of real butter on top... the perfect nautical nightcap. Best served in a pannikin, or tin cup.

Hunky-Dory - phrase meaning everything is okay coined from the name of the street Honki-Dori in

Yokohama, Japan, which catered to the pleasures of sailors.

India Pale Ale - type of beer developed in England in the late 18th century to survive the temperatures and rolling seas during the long sea voyage to India. The beer actually fermented during transit and the increased alcohol and hops served as preservatives.

Mai-Tai - exotic drink which in Tahitian literally means "out of this world." It was first mixed at Trader Vic's in San Francisco and gained its legendary status as a seagoing beverage while being served on passenger vessels to and from Hawaii.

Margarita - it is said that the Margarita is not a libation—it's a lifestyle. Largely due to Jimmy Buffett, it has become the concoction most associated with Caribbean cruising. There are countless variations of this tequila and lime cocktail, all of which are good.

"Mind Your Ps and Qs" - phrase meaning to be on good behavior that has its origin in sailors running a tab of pints and quarts in waterfront watering holes.

Nelson's Blood - Royal Navy slang for rum or grog stemming from the popular belief that Lord Nelson's body was placed into a barrel of rum for preservation after he was killed by a sniper at the Battle of Trafalgar.

Legend has it that sailors on the ship drank from the cask containing the body and gave birth to the phrase, "Tapping the Admiral."

Passing the Port - One of the most unique and practiced nautical customs is serving port after dinner for toasting. The decanter or bottle is passed only to the left and must never rest on the table until the last glass is charged (whether that person drinks or not). As the bottles are emptied, the person holding an empty bottle must raise it to indicate that a replacement is needed. When a bottle has reached the end of the table and the last glass is charged, it may be set down. How this custom originated is subject to considerable debate. Some historians believe that the custom of passing port to the left started in the British Royal Navy, where the word "port" meant left. Others are advocates of the theory that passing clockwise signifies the direction of the sun. Regardless, the stopper must remain out until the end of the evening.

Port - the choice of port as a nautical beverage has its origins in the 18th century when Britain and France were always at war. In Britain, to drink French wines was deemed unpatriotic. Instead, port, wine from ally Portugal (actually from the seaport Oporto), was substituted. Unlike normal wine, port is fortified by adding grape brandy during the fermentation process. This makes it more stable during temperature changes and allows it to last longer during sea travel.

Rum - the origins of rum as the standard seagoing libation started when the British captured the island of Jamaica in 1687. The name comes from *Saccharum*, the Latin word for sugar (rum is distilled from sugar cane). By 1731, this unspoilable commodity was added to the "Regulations and Instructions Relating to His Majesties Service at Sea" in the measure of a half-pint per sailor per day. The issuing of straight rum in half-pint quantities led to drunkenness and disciplinary problems. By 1740, water was added to the rum to make grog and the servings were spaced out over the day.

Rum Ration - a tot of grog, the equivalent of three gulps. The naval rum used by the Royal Navy was around 95 proof, and was cut with water. In the U.S. Navy the rum ration was changed to a whiskey ration in 1806 and was ended altogether on September 1, 1862.

Rum & Tonic - this could be to sail racing what a mint julep is to the Kentucky Derby. The preferred rum for many is Mount Gay, which has become synonymous with sailing (they sponsor many sailing regattas—the reason for all those red caps). Mix for taste, stir with a marlinespike and serve with a lime. Legend has it that Mount Gay Rum became the sailors' drink of choice in the 18th century because it proved their sailing skill. Barbados was considered the most difficult island from which to return to the European mainland (because of the prevailing winds and ocean currents), and sailors had to prove they had been there. A barrel of Mount Gay Rum was testament to that fact, and became the hallmark of superior sailors everywhere.

Schooner - a large goblet or drinking glass used for lager beer or ale.

Shanghai - to abduct a sailor by force. The term likely originated in the Chinese port of Shanghai where tea clippers in need of crewmen had saloon owners slip drunken sailors drugs in their drinks.

Shanties - work songs with marked rhythm, usually sung by a group of sailors while hoisting sail or anchor or pushing the capstan. More often than not they, along with sailor songs, included drinking references or were themselves entirely about the drinking. Among the better known "drinking" shanties are *The Drunken Sailor* and *Whisky Johnnie*.

"Splice the Main Brace" - an invitation to have a drink. It is widely believed that the phrase comes from rewarding the crew with an extra ration of rum after they performed a difficult chore, such as splicing the main brace.

"Suck the Monkey" or "Bleed the Monkey" - to sur-reptitiously draw liquor out of a cask with a straw. The phrase comes from the original practice of filling empty coconuts with alcohol, the three dark marks on the coconut resembling the face of a monkey.

"Sun over the Yardarm" - saying to indicate that it is time for a drink. It was generally assumed that in north-ern latitudes the sun would show above the foreyard of a ship by 1100, which was approximately the time on many ships of the forenoon "stand-easy," when many officers would slip below for their first drink of the day.

Sundowner - a refreshing mixed drink taken at the end of the day while observing the setting sun. Usually a pre-dinner drink made with no-nonsense ingredients, it requires a big glass and lots of ice.

"Tapping the Admiral" - to have a nip on the sly. It stems from the legend that Lord Nelson's body was pre-served in rum. See "Nelson's Blood."

"Three Sheets to the Wind!" - phrase describing some-one who has had too much to drink. Like a drunk, the reference is to a ship in disarray with its sheets flapping loosely in the breeze.

"Torpedo Juice" - slang for a submariner's beverage of

pure grain alcohol (fuel used for a torpedo's motor) with flavoring.

Tot - term for the daily ration of rum.

Up Spirits - shipboard pipe that announced the daily issue of rum, usually at 1600. At seven bells (1530), grog would be pumped. At eight bells, the crew would knock off ship's work. The rum ration had to be drunk on the spot.

Wetting Down - informal ceremony hosted by a newly commissioned or recently promoted military officer where he or she is toasted by others and picks up the bar tab. It is advised to bring a powerful thirst when invited to one of these functions.

Wine-Dark Sea - description of the Mediterranean, comes from the *Iliad* translated by Andrew Lang, Walter Leaf and Ernest Myers, and from *The Odyssey* translated by Andrew Lang and Samuel Henry Butcher.

Sailor Slang

The rich tradition of drinking and sailing live on in our lexicon. The truth is that many men chose a life at sea in order to get liquor and to have drinking companions. Below is a sampling of sailor slang for having tipped one too many. If you're so described by any of these you'll know you're one drink away from a tattoo:

Admiral of the narrow seas

Beyond Salvage

Bilged

Blind

Canned to the crow's nest

Capsized

Cargoed

Carrying too much sail

Carrying two/three red lights

Channels under

Chock-a-block

Cockbilled

Drunk as a drowned rat

Drunk as a lord

Filled to the gills

Foggy

Green about the gills

Grogged

Groggy

Half-seas over

Keelhauled

Loaded to the gunwales

Loaded to the Plimsoll mark

Oiled as an Exxon tanker captain

On beam's end

One over the eight

Over the bay

Pickled

Piscatorically drunk

Pooped

Popeyed/ Pop-eyed

Right before the wind with all studding sails out

Screwed, blued and tattooed

Shipwrecked

Slewed

Sloshed

Soggy

Soogeying the bulkhead

Sprung

Stewed to the gills

Taking on fuel

Three sheets to the wind

Up the creek

Under the weather

Varnished

Waterlogged

With decks awash

Wrecked

Aboard ship, rum had value just like money and personal debts were paid with it. This remuneration came in different denominations: A "wet" was just enough to cover the lips; a "sipper" was a "gentlemanly" sip; a "gulper" was one big swallow; and, "Sandy Bottoms" (sounding much like a character on "Spongebob Squarepants") involved drinking the entire contents of another's tot.

Numerous Nautically-Named Libations

Grog could very well have been the world's first cocktail and ever since few things have been more intertwined than boats and mixed drinks. Following is a selection of nautical cocktails listed alphabetically. Before mixing it's best to consult your favorite bartender's guide.

America's Cup, Barbary Coast, Bay Breeze, Beachcomber, Beach House, Bermuda Highball, Blue Dolphin, Blue Whale, Boat Drink, Boston Tea Party, Brass Monkey, Captain Crunch, Caribbean Punch, Diesel Fuel, Fart in the Ocean, Flying Dutchman, Fog Cutter, Fog Horn, Havana Cocktail, Hawaiian Cocktail, High Tide, Honolulu Cocktail, Honolulu Hammer, Hurricane, Jamaican Coffee, Kamikaze, Lady Hamilton, Lifesaver, Long Island Iced Tea, Mai Tai, Nantucket, Navy Grog, Nelson's Blood, Outrigger, Pearl Harbor, Pimm's Cup, Pina Colada, Pineapple Cocktail, Planter's Punch, Real McCoy, Reef Juice, Riviera, Rum Runner, SS Manhattan, Sailing By, Sailor's Quaff, Smooth Sailing, Salty Dog, Sea Breeze, Searchlight, Sex on the Beach, Sex on the Boat, Sunset Horizon, Tall Ship,

Tropical Storm, Waikiki Beachcomber, Yellow Submarine, Yacht Club.

And for those so inclined, there are a host of shooters...

Beach Ball, Blue Marlin, Exxon Valdez, Fisherman's Wharf, Flaming Depth Charge, Great White Shark, Depth Charge, Harbor Lights, Jelly Fish, Johnny on the Beach, Oil Slick, Oyster Shooter, Sand in Your Butt, Sea Monkey, Sex on the Beach, Sex With The Captain, Sun and Surf, Sub-Tactical Nuclear Warhead, South Seas Rampage.

While hoisting a few drinks in the rough and tumble waterfront bars sailors had to be on constant lookout for danger. The pewter mugs they drank from were fashioned with glass bottoms so that they could keep an eye on things, even while imbibing. Quite a few of them are believed to have uttered, "Here's looking at you!" before quaffing a beer.

What Do You Do With A Drunken Sailor?

Cautions of Drinking and Boating

Drinking while boating is illegal, but venturing out on the water even after moderate social drinking, can be very hazardous.

A Story:

Two sailors, drinking alcohol and through the haze of the day, thought they spotted what, according to their assumed position, was Block Island, Rhode Island (which they had never seen) some miles off to the south of them. One commented, "geez, no wonder they call it Block Island, it looks just like a block!" Being ahead of schedule they decided to sail to Block Island for an overnighter and started to sail toward it. They just never seemed to get any closer—even after four or five hours. As the haze lifted, and the visibility cleared, their view of Block Island, the island they just couldn't seem to get any closer to, became unmistakable. Their "Block Island" turned out to be a barge loaded with shipping containers on the deck, that they had been chasing in their haze for hours.

All boaters needs to understand the risks of boating under the influence of alcohol or drugs (BUI). It is illegal to operate a boat while under the influence of alcohol or drugs in every state. The U.S. Coast Guard also enforces a federal law that prohibits BUI. This law pertains to ALL boats (from canoes and rowboats to the largest ships)—and includes foreign vessels that operate in U.S. waters, as well as U.S. vessels on the high seas.

Alcohol is the most destabilizing force any vessel can have. And water is a poor chaser. Many boater's do not allow drinking on board while underway (which may be why so many boats never leave the dock). Other skippers allow one beer for every adult on board when racing, broken out only when the finishing gun sounds, thus there is strong incentive to get back to the dock. Whatever your methods, please, keep it on an even keel!